Managing

Operations

**YOUR SELF-
DEVELOPMENT
ACTION PLAN**

PETER GRAINGER

 NP
Kogan Page Ltd, London
Nichols Publishing Company,
New Jersey

First published in 1994

Apart from any fair dealing for the purposes of research or
private study, or criticism, as permitted under the Copyright,
Designs and Patents Act, 1988, this publication may only be
reproduced, stored or transmitted, in any form or by any means,
with the prior permission in writing of the publishers, or in the
case of reprographic reproduction in accordance with the terms of
licences issued by the Copyright Licensing Agency. Enquiries
concerning reproduction outside those terms should be sent to the
publishers at the undermentioned address:

Kogan Page Limited
120 Pentonville Road
London N1 9JN

© Peter Grainger, 1994

Published in the United States of America by Nichols Publishing,
PO Box 6036, East Brunswick, New Jersey 08816

British Library Cataloguing in Publication Data

A CIP record for this book is available from the British Library.

ISBN (UK) 0 7494 1251 8
ISBN (US) 0-89397-433-1

Typeset by the author
Printed and bound in Great Britain by Biddles Ltd, Guildford and
King's Lynn.

CONTENTS

Preface   **5**

Introduction   **7**
   The approach *8*
   The toolkit of skills *10*
   The MCI links *14*
   The method of learning *18*

1. Personal Development   **20**
   The culture *21*
   The Pygmalion Effect *24*
   Personal style *28*
   Style profile *34*

2. Clarifying Roles   **41**
   Having a purpose *42*
   Giving it shape *44*
   Writing it down *48*
   Talking it over *52*
   Summary worksheets *54*
   Links to other skills *58*

3. Specifying Targets and Standards   59
Clarifying targets *60*
Defining standards *64*
Involving others *66*
Summary worksheets *70*
Links to other skills *74*

4. Planning Action   75
Identifying options *76*
Making it visible *80*
Setting priorities *82*
Making it happen *86*
Summary worksheets *90*
Links to other skills *94*

Index   95

PREFACE

It has taken more than 20 years to refine the 12 generic skills of management, which are the foundation of the Manager's Toolkit series, into a form which is both straightforward enough for busy managers to learn and which actually works in real life.

The skills contained in the original *Manager's Toolkit* manual and the linked style definitions were developed in the course of 15 years' management experience in senior training and development positions with Rank Xerox. Unique opportunities existed in the company at that time for creative approaches to the training and development of first-level and middle managers on both sides of the Atlantic.

As a member of a number of specialist teams in the USA and Europe, I was fortunate to come into personal contact with many of the most effective management techniques of recent times – for example, the systematic approach of Charles Kepner and Ben Tregoe and the Huthwaite Research Group's 'Interactive Skills'.

The first step was to build these techniques into a set of 'Management Standards' which the management teams of Rank Xerox's manufacturing plants in the UK developed over a number of years, and then test them in *practical* situations, including residential training programmes.

Every manager participating in a training programme brought a real-life problem to the course, and the skills taught were applied to each of those 'issues' during the programme. If a technique did not work or took too long to apply, it was discarded or modified.

After ten years of running intensive management development programmes at all levels, we had so refined the techniques that they could be integrated into a comprehensive 'toolkit' of skills that would actually guarantee results (pages 10–12).

At this time, my later business partner, Roger Acland, and I developed the personal style definitions which became an essential ingredient of all our work, and from which I later created the 'Personal Development Toolkit' and the Style Profile (page 37).

This integrated learning approach, built upon the need for positive thinking (page 26), has proved its special value to groups of managers and potential managers drawn from a wide range of organizations, from students, accountants, and engineers to teams in Allied Lyons, Rank Xerox and British Telecom.

The great benefit of the approach is that it is quick to use, flexible – *and it works*. After years of practical application, the 12 skills have now been honed to such simple effectiveness that they can be readily acquired through open learning. Look through the structure and methodology of the book to see how the approach works in practice for the three 'Operations' skills contained in this manual.

I believe the hundreds of organizations of all sizes that have purchased the original *Manager's Toolkit* manual since its publication in 1992 provide ample confirmation of the simple effectiveness of both the content and the method of learning.

Peter Grainger

INTRODUCTION

1. The approach   Page   8

2. The toolkit of skills   Page   10

3. The MCI links   Page   14

4. The method of learning   Page   18

INTRODUCTION

1. The approach

The Manager's Toolkit series is designed to be suitable for a wide range of managers. You may already be a manager responsible for the work of other people and want to learn how to make more of yourself and the resources under your control. You may be facing the prospect of the responsibility of managing – or you may want to take an opportunity to manage when it arises – and be uncertain how to set about it.

To make the most of the books in the series you will either not have received any management training or the training you have received will have only given you *knowledge* of management and not the practical skills of *how* to manage.

Statistics show that few managers have received any formal training. I suspect most managers are too busy – or too exhausted – to find time to study 'management' literature. The style of each book in the series is therefore as economical and as visual as possible, concentrating on making clear each step of each process or skill – more like a DIY car manual than a learned business treatise.

The series will not only explain the essential generic skills of managing yourself and others but will give you opportunities to *practise* those skills as you apply them to your own real-life situations. The comprehensive Index on pages 95 and 96 provides you with easy access when you have a specific skills need.

In addition to acquiring such essential skills as specifying targets and standards and chairing meetings, you will come to understand yourself better, the person behind the manager or potential manager.

Some people master some of the skills of management more readily than others because of the sort of *person* they are. Some people are good with information but not with people, others are good with people but poor at taking action.

You will analyse your *personal style* in relation to three style definitions and as a result determine which are the most important skills for you personally to work on (see pages 38–9). You can therefore create your own development plan from the moment you buy the first book, confident that you are using your learning time most effectively.

Finally, you will gradually build up a *positive approach* to the situations in which you find yourself as a manager. Developing positive expectations of people and situations is a critical part of leadership and management. It has to be acquired and continuously worked at. It is not just a matter of attitude, but of applying particular techniques. Anyone can learn these techniques and so make a remarkable difference not only to the way they manage but also to the impact they make on the world about them.

2. The toolkit of skills

The Manager's Toolkit series consists of four personal development workbooks designed as open learning training and development aids to enable anyone who wants to be able to manage – or manage better – to acquire the necessary skills in their own time and at their own pace.

The series is based on the single volume *The Manager's Toolkit*, which I published in 1992, and was bought by large numbers of human resource specialists in large and small organizations throughout the United Kingdom. It was felt that making the *Toolkit* available *as a series* in a smaller format at lower cost would bring it within reach of individual managers and potential managers as and when they required each group of skills.

The concept of an *integrated* 'toolkit' of skills provides you with the opportunity to use the skills in sequence (for example in a major project), or skill-by-skill according to your personal need.

The formation of the toolkit shown opposite was the basis of the original *Manager's Toolkit*. The 12 key skills emerged from more complex models, and in numerical sequence represent a sequential, cyclical *process of management*, from clarifying roles (1) to giving and receiving feedback (12).

Each skill is not only important in its own right, but also links with its neighbour in making up *clusters* of skills for particular purposes, for example in this model to provide a

The Toolkit of Skills

a process of management

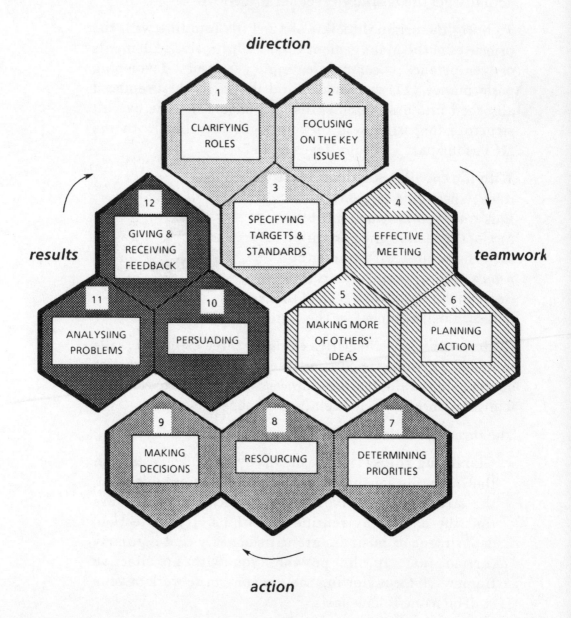

direction

1 CLARIFYING ROLES

2 FOCUSING ON THE KEY ISSUES

3 SPECIFYING TARGETS & STANDARDS

4 EFFECTIVE MEETING

12 GIVING & RECEIVING FEEDBACK

results

teamwork

11 ANALYSIING PROBLEMS

10 PERSUADING

5 MAKING MORE OF OTHERS' IDEAS

6 PLANNING ACTION

9 MAKING DECISIONS

8 RESOURCING

7 DETERMINING PRIORITIES

action

© *PETER GRAINGER 1994*

sense of *direction*, to make the most of a group, ie *teamwork*, to make things happen, ie *action,* or to make sure you do actually get the *results* you set out to achieve.

To bring the original toolkit of 12 skills into line with the priorities of the Management Charter Initiative's 'elements of competence', 'communicating' (7) and 'developing performance' (11) were added and the skills they replaced absorbed into associated skills (see page 11). The overall structure (opposite) was then brought into line with the MCI's four-part 'key roles' (see page 17).

With the *operations* skills of 'clarifying roles', 'specifying targets and stand-ards' and 'planning action' at the core of the toolkit, the particular skills associated with managing *people, resources* and *information* link conveniently with each of them to form a toolkit model for the series.

resources   people   ops   information

Each workbook in the series explores three essential skills in depth, providing opportunities for *open learning* practice at each step of the learning process. The process, common to all the workbooks, is explained on pages 18–19.

The three 'operations' skills covered by this volume are:

- **Clarifying roles** (1) is the means by which you establish the inter-relationship of jobs within your organization, the structure that gives you the machinery to ensure that the day-to-day routine operations of your section, department or business are satisfactorily and regularly carried out. It also provides you with an effective framework for reviewing the *total on-going* work of your staff on a one-to-one basis.

The Manager's Toolkit Series

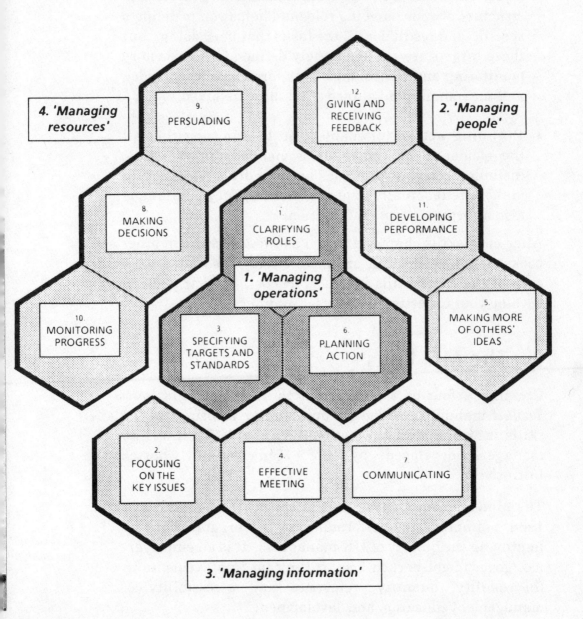

4. 'Managing resources'

2. 'Managing people'

9. PERSUADING

12. GIVING AND RECEIVING FEEDBACK

8. MAKING DECISIONS

1. CLARIFYING ROLES

11. DEVELOPING PERFORMANCE

1. 'Managing operations'

10. MONITORING PROGRESS

3. SPECIFYING TARGETS AND STANDARDS

6. PLANNING ACTION

5. MAKING MORE OF OTHERS' IDEAS

2. FOCUSING ON THE KEY ISSUES

4. EFFECTIVE MEETING

7. COMMUNICATING

3. 'Managing information'

© PETER GRAINGER 1994

- **Specifying targets and standards** (3) links your objectives or short-term improvement targets to the structure of your on-going role, and helps you to define a specific 'end result' for all the tasks that need doing. But these targets are not adequately defined for satisfactory monitoring and control until standards have been added and the commitment gained of all those involved .

- **Planning action** (6) enables you to bring together all the elements that make up a visible plan of action, including relevant priorities and the drive necessary to make sure it actually happens. Contingency planning is also incorporated into this section.

After each skills chapter a model shows the skills in other books in the series that are most closely associated with each of the three skills in this workbook, so that you can develop your expertise in a focused manner.

3. The MCI links

Creating a four-part series from the original *Manager's Toolkit* manual provided an opportunity to bring the 12 skills into line with the national standards for first line managers developed by the Management Charter Initiative.

The Management Charter Initiative (MCI) was formed in 1988 'to improve the performance of UK organisations by improving the quality of UK managers'. It is an employer-led, government-backed body calling for improvements in the quality, quantity, relevance and accessibility of management education and development.

After extensive consultation, research and testing, the MCI is establishing a framework of four levels for management and supervisory development (Supervisory, Certificate, Diploma and Masters), with assessments based on demonstrated ability to manage. The guidelines at each of these levels give clear guidance on what is expected of managers at different levels, providing specific requirements for their development and assessment.

Detailed standards have been established for Supervisors, First Level Managers and Middle Managers, and I have taken the *First Level Management Standards* as the most appropriate link to the skills in the Manager's Toolkit series. They provide the management reference point for the National Vocational Qualifications at Level 4.

The standards first break down the key *roles* of management into *units* and *elements of competence*. Those covered in this workbook are:

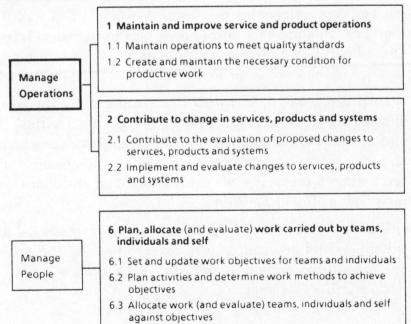

Manage Operations

1 Maintain and improve service and product operations

1.1 Maintain operations to meet quality standards

1.2 Create and maintain the necessary condition for productive work

2 Contribute to change in services, products and systems

2.1 Contribute to the evaluation of proposed changes to services, products and systems

2.2 Implement and evaluate changes to services, products and systems

Manage People

6 Plan, allocate (and evaluate) work carried out by teams, individuals and self

6.1 Set and update work objectives for teams and individuals

6.2 Plan activities and determine work methods to achieve objectives

6.3 Allocate work (and evaluate) teams, individuals and self against objectives

Managing Resources has been broadened beyond 'manage finance' to cover *all resources* and includes 'making decisions', a skill which is essential to 'contribute to the recruitment and selection of personnel' (*Unit 4, opposite*).

The first three elements of Unit 6 (see page 15) have been included in this book because they link especially well with clarifying roles, tasks and plans.

The focus of *operations* activities for the MCI (*Units 1 and 2, opposite*) is '*maintain* and *improve service* and product operations' and 'contribute to the *implementation* of *change* in services, products and systems'.

Notice the words I have put in italics – operations is about *maintaining, improving* and *implementing*. You will find therefore an emphasis in this book on *improvement* targets and identifying options, as well as on maintaining the *routines* of the work to be done.

Elements 6.1–6.3, linked with Units 1 and 2, are the *means* of maintaining and implementing (eg 'plan activities', 'set and update work objectives' and 'determine work methods'), and are most appropriately covered in this book. The remaining dimensions of 'evaluation' and 'feedback' are included in *Managing People*.

Other MCI references, for example to 'work methods' and 'schedules and procedures', are covered here by the *process* or *procedure* activities within each role's area of responsibility (see page 50).

MCI key roles and units of competence for first line managers

Manage Operations

1 *Maintain and improve service and product operations*

2 *Contribute to the implementation of change in services, products and systems*

Manage Finance

3 Recommend, monitor and control the use of resources

Manage Resources

4 Contribute to the recruitment and selection of personnel

Manage People

5 Develop teams, individuals and self to enhance performance

6 *Plan, allocate* (and evaluate) *work carried out by teams, individuals and self*

7 Create, maintain and enhance effective working relationships

Manage Information

8 Seek, evaluate and organize information for action

9 Exchange information to solve problems and make decisions

Crown Copyright © 1989-1992 inclusive

'Corrective action' is covered by contingency planning (page 88) and 'monitoring' by the emphasis placed throughout on adequate standards. 'Communication' and 'consultation' are stressed throughout this book, along with the importance of developing dialogue with both internal and external customers.

4. The method of learning

The book is laid out with explanations of each skill on the left and blank forms on the right for you to complete step-by-step in parallel with each explanation. You will find it helpful to read through *the whole* of the explanation for each chapter on the left before starting to complete the practice forms on the right, in order to see each step in its context.

In the practice forms on the right you will always be asked for information from *your own work situation*, so that the effort you put in will be repaid by consistently providing you with practical material for use on the job. At the bottom of each box on every practice sheet you will find sample answers to guide you towards your own answer.

The explanation and practice sheets for each of the three skills are followed first by a completed worksheet and then by an identical blank worksheet for you to fill in for yourself.

These worksheets are designed to pull together all the steps of each process and to act as a summary of the skill you have just worked through. They are also useful reminders of each skill as you look for opportunities to practise each of them as appropriate occasions arise.

The process works like this:

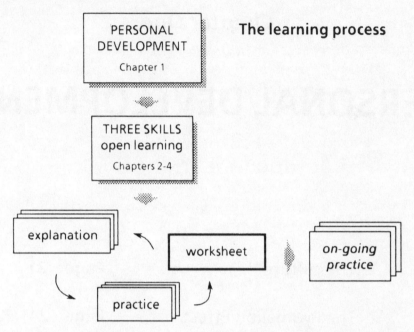

After the open learning practice available in this book, first section-by-section, step-by-step, and then on each summary worksheet, *immediate practice* at work to secure the skills is most important. But valuable practice opportunities also exist *outside* the working environment in low risk domestic or social situations.

You may for example be chair or secretary of a social or sporting committee – do you know what you are really responsible for? Have you ever wished you had explained more clearly to a builder exactly what you wanted him to do? I once discovered how much easier it is to cope with a family wedding when you have a plan that's written down!

You do not learn to drive a car or to play the piano without *regular practice* – learning the skills of management has just the same requirement.

Chapter One

PERSONAL DEVELOPMENT

1. The culture   Page   21

2. The Pygmalion Effect   Page   24

3. Personal style   Page   28

4. Style profile   Page   34

PERSONAL DEVELOPMENT

1. The culture

The management climate and culture at work is critical to successful personal development. The role model we provide for our staff or the example of operational behaviour that our manager sets for us creates an environment that can make or break our willingness and our ability to develop ourselves.

Management today is in danger of losing its entrepreneurial excitement – it is becoming too cerebral and too constrained, too concerned with systems and procedures and too careful not to make mistakes. Stress at work has increased as risk-taking and the means by which real improvement can be achieved are consistently constrained. We have forgotten that management and finding new ways to do things better can actually be *fun*!

Improvement, an essential part of the MCI's standards relating to 'operations', can so easily be seen *defensively* as putting the things right that have gone wrong. Instead improvement should be about creatively finding new solutions to old problems. It should be about coming to work each day excited by the prospect of finding better ways of actually making things happen. I wonder when you last felt that creative excitement!

Improvement should mean constantly trying to meet our customers' requirements more quickly and at lower cost – and *enjoying* the experience. The excitement will then transmit itself to those around us as *enthusiasm*. It is this focused enthusiasm that is the vital ingredient of a management that actually makes things happen.

Improvement is also about *involvement*. It is asking people who do the job for their ideas about how it might be done better, and involving them day-by-day in the evolving success of the business. While it has been one of the continuing explanations of Japan's industrial success, in Britain we experienced temporary enchantment with 'Quality Circles' in the 1980s, and then failed to exploit the best parts of the process for our own business culture.

Training employees from directors to shop-floor personnel in group problem-solving techniques has convinced me of the extent to which *everyone* can contribute valuable suggestions for improvement, if only they are asked as a regular routine of management

And how many of us really know what we are supposed to be doing? We may be very clear about the latest crisis task, but do we have an overview of our *total* job and of our *total* performance? Clarifying roles and tasks (the foundation of this manual) and then regularly reviewing individual performance on a one-to-one basis has at last become part of good management practice in larger organizations. But I believe it is so critical to motivation and controlled performance that it should by now be as much part of all businesss operations as a computer or a set of accounts.

To perform effectively we need the freedom and the tools to develop our *own* challenging targets. Involvement in setting standards encourasges people to aim high, to feel responsible for their own performance and that they can be trusted to monitor their own work for themselves.

And of course everyone needs to know what the others with whom they work are supposed to be doing, *their* mission and their standards. Operational cooperation is critical to success, and is the reason why it is so important to have roles, standards and joint action plans written down and shared – however informally.

With the customer – internal as well as external – increasingly determining workload and standards, I believe the role of the traditional operations manager will gradually change. In time he or she will become a *facilitator*, an arbiter, a resource provider and a coach, asisting team members continuously to meet agreed customer requirements more quickly and at lower cost. It is an attractive scenario to many people, and one that provides great opportunities for personal development.

The self-teach open learning method of this workbook will help you to take increasing responsibility for *your own* operating results and the level of your own personal performance. It will allow you to develop your own skills as and when you need them, in your own time and at your own pace. Performance will then continuously improve in a culture in which serving customers and successfully competing with competitors will be a normal and enjoyable way fo life. We have a little way to go!

2. The Pygmalion Effect

The way management is performed around us creates a culture in which we feel able – or not – to develop our full potential. Similarly the right *attitude* is critical to managing ourselves and other people, and the development of a *positive* attitude is required before setting out to acquire particular skills. Understanding the Pygmalion Effect is a major step in the right direction.

The essence of the Pygmalion Effect lies in the power of positive *expectations*. The word 'Pygmalion' comes not from George Bernard Shaw but from Greek mythology. Pygmalion was a sculptor in Cyprus who carved a statue of a girl which was so beautiful that he fell in love with it. So powerful were his expectations and his will that Venus stepped in and turned the statue into human form – and they both lived happily ever after!

Positive thinking has been proved to be critical to success; positive expectations of an outcome increase the likelihood of a successful result. The conscious development of positive thinking and of high expectations of ourselves and others can have a remarkable effect on our confidence, our relationships and our success.

And yet the most natural response to unknown people and uncertain situations is *negative*. So often, both individually and in groups, we display negative rather than positive responses. Often it is because we are uncertain. Uncertainty leads to fear and fear to expectations of failure – a self-fulfilling prophecy.

2. The Pygmalion Effect

2.1 Write down a difficult situation with which you have recently had to deal:

I had to investigate a complaint from a customer

2.2 What was your attitude to this situation when you approached it?	*I knew it would be difficult - he's complained before*
What was the effect of your attitude on what happened?	*I didn't expect it to be genuine. Staff didn't take it seriously*
2.3 If your approach was negative, how might you have been more positive towards the situation concerned?	*I should have been open-minded - might be genuine - he is a customer!*

To manage effectively we have consciously and continuously to fill the vacuum of uncertainty with positive expectations. We need to make a specific and conscious effort to identify the positive elements in any situation and the strengths of any individual. 'Is the glass half-full or half-empty?' *It is remarkable how easy it is to think of the positive factors in a situation if we just stop and consider for a moment.*

Once we have tried to be positive about situations and people, we can even try a little *enthusiasm*! Enthusiasm is an essential ingredient in getting things done successfully, particularly when we want help from other people. They may be suspicious at first, but they will find it difficult not to respond.

But positive thinking, and particularly enthusiasm, need to be *demonstrated* for the Pygmalion Effect to work. The influence we have on other people results directly from the way we behave towards them. If we are in the habit of treating people in a way that conveys trust and high expectations, a positive response, and so positive results, are likely to follow. A smile at the right moment can have a dramatic effect.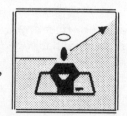

Confidence of course affects whether we manage situations positively or negatively. We require confidence in ourselves in order to have a positive effect on other people, and to have that confidence we need to *understand ourselves*, to be aware of our natural strengths and to recognize our limitations. The next section will enable you to do just that.

2.4 Write down a situation in the future that you are uncertain about, a situation where you don't know what is likely to happen:	*Appraisal with Margaret next Thursday*
2.5 What are your expectations of that situation? If your expectations are negative, how is it likely to affect the outcome?	*She'll complain about her job; she doesn't get on with Jim* *I'll be defensive - 'If she doesn't like the job, she can go'*
2.6 Think of the positive factors involved and how you could use them to make your expectations more positive.	*She has considerable experience; could we use it better?*

3. Personal style

Our ability to manage some situations and not others, to manage some people and not others, is partly a question of the sort of person we are, our personal style. If we understood more about our style it would help us to know and to develop our natural strengths and to accept or overcome our limitations.

The three styles we developed are very simple and represent the basis of 'what makes people tick'. They first emerged as a result of considering an interesting model of motivation, which exactly reflected the result of the research we were doing at the time into leadership styles and the means of identifying *potential* managers.

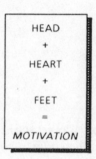

The first distinct style is **'Analyse'** (or 'Head') to represent the thinking, analytical type of person; the second is **'Bond'** (or 'Heart'), the feeling, caring type of person; the third is **'Command'** (or 'Feet'), the active, results-orientated type of person.

Each style can be summed up as follows:

'ANALYSE' (or 'Head')

Values logic and distrusts subjective judgements; able to provide considered and rational arguments; keen to see rules and procedures applied.

'BOND' (or 'Heart')

Conscious of the importance of mutual understanding and stresses the benefits of working with people; seeks to get the best out of others by trust and encouragement.

'COMMAND' (or 'Feet')

Likes to be in control of people and events, quickly responding to job demands and opportunities; trusts own judgement and acts on conclusions; inclined to use incentives and sanctions to influence results.

A high-scoring 'Analyse' type of person is likely to be quiet and methodical, a conscientious administrator who likes to get things right. A predominantly 'Bond' person is likely to be open with emotions and conscious of the importance of other people, a visible carer with individuals or inside a team. A 'Command' person is likely to be impatient for results and to know instinctively what needs doing, an entrepreneur or 'born organizer'.

But people rarely fit a style description exactly. People are usually a mixture of the three styles, generally of just two of them. *Few of us have the capacity to spread equally across all three.* We often have one which is an area of weakness which tends to ruin our all round performance, but which provides a focus for our personal development.

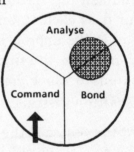

There are of course many current methods of identifying personal style. Generally, though, they provide you with an interesting profile but no plan of action to aid your development, and almost certainly no links to learnable management skills.

However, one of the benefits of the 'toolkit' approach is that the skills within the toolkit can be re-assembled into different shapes for different purposes. The skills in the Personal Development Toolkit overleaf have been re-assembled to match the most appropriate style.

'Analyse' covers the *information*-providing skills ('monitoring', 'clarifying', 'specifying' and 'focusing'), skills associated with individual thinking processes.

'Bond' covers skills associated with being with *people* ('making more of others' ideas', 'giving and receiving feedback', 'communicating' and 'meeting'), skills most effective when done with openness and feeling.

The 'Command' skills are all related to taking *action* and getting results ('persuading', 'planning action', 'making decisions' and 'developing performance').

In the style questionnaire overleaf you are asked to consider yourself in relation to 12 straightforward statements. How far does each statement represent a fair description of you? Circle the appropriate number against each statement, and then circle the number in the next column to indicate the extent to which you would like to change the rating you have given yourself.

At the centre of the personal development model opposite are the core skills of 'specifying targets and standards', 'making more of others' ideas' and 'planning action' (in italics). These are the essence of the integrated style – **'Drive'** – which contains elements of the other three styles. It is the basis of a balanced *leadership* – and of an effective management – style:

Clear and positive in thinking towards future possibilities; capable of generating enthusiasm and a flexible approach to achieving results; is sensitive to others' feelings and expectations and inspires teamwork.

'Drive' style requires the ability to move between 'Head', 'Heart' and 'Feet', to be able to adjust your personal style according to the changing needs of the situation.

Personal Development Toolkit

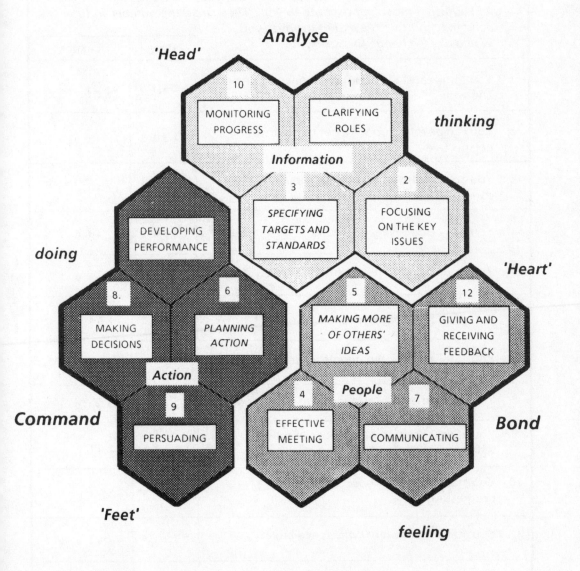

© PETER GRAINGER 1994

Style Questionnaire

3.1 Score the extent to which the following statements apply to you NOW on a scale 1–5 (1 = Not you; 3 = Yes, but...; 5 = Fully you). Circle the number (1 2 3 4 5) which is most appropriate to you. Then circle the number in the next column to indicate the extent to which you would like to change this rating:

	'NOW'	'CHANGE'
1. You think carefully about what needs doing and why.	1 2 **3** 4 5	+2 **+1** 0 -1 -2
2. You can be relied upon to get things into perspective.	1 2 3 **4** 5	+2 +1 **0** -1 -2
3. You are concerned that things should be done correctly.	1 **2** 3 4 5	**+2** +1 0 -1 -2
4. You work effectively in groups.	1 2 3 **4** 5	+2 **+1** 0 -1 -2
5. You respond positively to other people's ideas.	1 2 3 **4** 5	+2 +1 **0** -1 -2
6. You get people organized for action.	1 2 **3** 4 5	**+2** +1 0 -1 -2
7. You consistently keep people informed.	1 2 **3** 4 5	+2 **+1** 0 -1 -2
8. You have no difficulty making up your mind.	1 2 **3** 4 5	+2 **+1** 0 -1 -2
9. You always seem to be able to get others to do what you want.	1 2 **3** 4 5	+2 **+1** 0 -1 -2
10. You make sure you know how things are progressing.	1 2 **3** 4 5	**+2** +1 0 -1 -2
11. You make the most of what is available.	1 2 **3** 4 5	+2 **+1** 0 -1 -2
12. You prefer to deal with people face-to-face.	1 2 3 4 **5**	+2 +1 **0** -1 -2

Bold type represents the scores in the example on page 35.   © *PETER GRAINGER 1994*

3.2   To consider your own relationship to the three basic styles transfer your 'Now' scores and the 'Change' scores from the questionnaire according to the number of each statement.   Add up the total 'Now' scores and highlight the most significant 'Change' scores, keeping the two sets separate:

		'NOW' SCORES	'CHANGE' SCORES

'Analyse'

1. You think carefully about what needs doing and why.   [   ] *3*   [   ] *+1*

3. You are concerned that things should be done correctly.   [   ] *2*   [   ] (*+2*)

10. You make sure you know how things are progressing.   [   ] *3*   [   ] (*+2*)

2. You can be relied upon to get things into perspective.   [   ] *4*   [   ] *0*

TOTAL [   ] *12*

'Bond'

7. You consistently keep people informed.   [   ] *3*   [   ] *+1*

12. You prefer to deal with people face-to-face.   [   ] *5*   [   ] *0*

5. You respond positively to other people's ideas.   [   ] *4*   [   ] *0*

4. You work effectively in groups.   [   ] *4*   [   ] *+1*

TOTAL [   ] *16*

'Command'

9. You always seem to be able to get others to do what you want.   [   ] *4*   [   ] *+1*

6. You get people organized for action.   [   ] *3*   [   ] (*+2*)

8. You have no difficulty making up your mind.   [   ] *3*   [   ] *+1*

11. You make the most of what is available.   [   ] *4*   [   ] *+1*

TOTAL [   ] *14*

Example scores are in **bold type**; the resulting profile appears on Page 35.

4. Style profile

You should now have a total score for each style, but these totals do not tell you very much until you see them graphically in relation to each other. It is this inter-relationship that is important, not the size of the totals produced.

By transferring your total scores for 'Analyse', 'Bond' and 'Command' on to the model on page 37 your profile will normally emerge as a triangle with a 'pull' towards one particular area of skills. (The letters 'AB', 'BA' etc will help you to communicate the direction of that pull to others.)

In the example opposite the person's *strengths* lie to the bottom right towards 'Bond'. The skills in that area are 'making more of others' ideas', 'communicating' and 'giving and receiving feedback'. The area on the *opposite* side to the shape of the profile (shaded) covers skills from AB to CA. These are likely to be among the skills to concentrate on as personal development priorities.   'Clarifying roles' and 'specifying targets and standards' are of course covered in this workbook.

If the triangle of your profile is equilateral you are probably 'Drive' style, or at least have the potential to be. But it is more likely that there will be a 'pull' in one particular direction, a 'skew' towards one style or perhaps two. This skew will be in the direction of your *natural* strengths, and the skills on the model *nearest* to that skew will identify a particular area of confidence and competence for you.

Example of Completed Style Profile

4.1 Write your total 'Now' scores for each 'style' from 3.2 on page 33 in the boxes below:

'Analyse':   'Bond':   'Command':

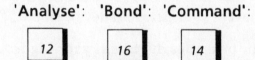

| 12 | 16 | 14 |

Circle or cross the appropriate number on the model below, and join up the points to produce a style profile. Then highlight the skills with the highest 'Change' scores:

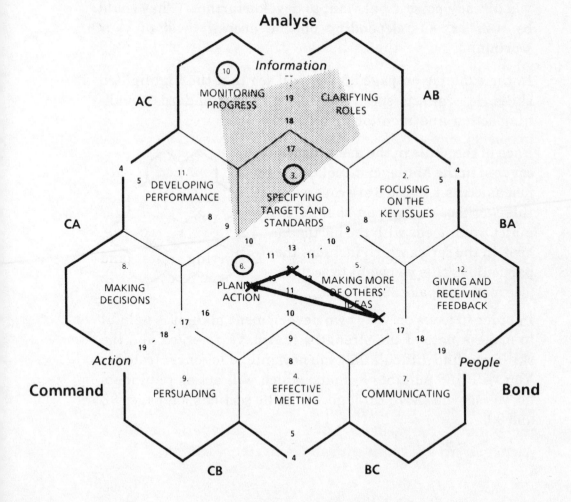

© *PETER GRAINGER 1994*

The skills on the model *furthest away* from the shape of your profile are those that you probably do not find easy to carry out; you may therefore need to concentrate on them particularly as part of your personal development.

To check out your priorities, highlight your highest 'Change' scores from Section 3.2 on page 33 by ringing or underlining the appropriate number on the model opposite. These may be skills which you find difficult and want to improve or skills you already possess but want to develop further. (They could be +2s or +1s depending on the overall level of your scoring.)

In the example on page 35 you will see that the highlighted skills (ie +2s) are 'specifying targets and standards', 'planning action' and 'monitoring progress'.

Each of the skills in the model opposite is covered in the Manager's Toolkit series, just as skills 1, 3 and 6 are covered in this workbook. You can therefore match your needs with the particular book in the series which includes the particular skills you want to acquire (see model on page 39).

In order to focus on your own development plan, it is helpful to make a note of the strengths that have emerged and the skills you find difficult that you now intend to concentrate on. You will find suitable formats, which will act as reminders for you as you move through the skills sections, on pages 38 and 39.

Style Profile

4.2 Write your total 'Now' scores for each 'style' from 3.2 on page 33 in the boxes below:

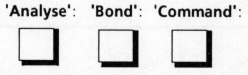

'Analyse':   'Bond':   'Command':

Circle or cross the appropriate number on the model below, and join up the points to produce a style profile. Then highlight the skills with the highest 'Change' scores:

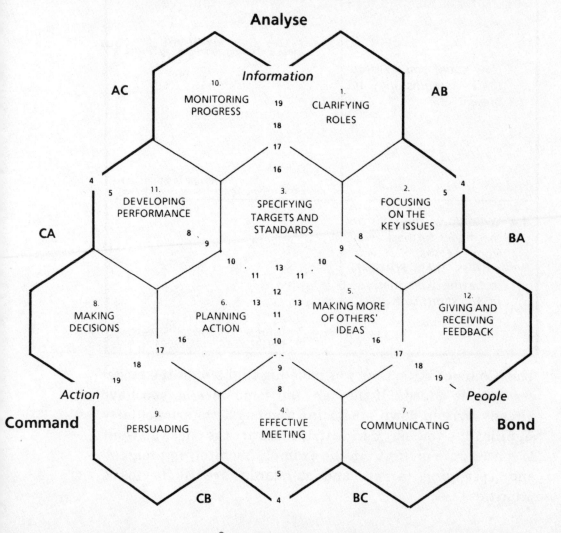

© PETER GRAINGER 1994

From consideration of your profile, identify your strongest skills in the space below and consider ways of developing them. Then make a note of the skills furthest away from the shape of your profile, and confirm that these are the skills you want to improve.

4.3 *Write down the skills closest to the shape of your profile. These are likely to be your natural strengths:* *How could you develop these strengths in your present job?*	*Making more of others' ideas and giving and receiving feedback* *In one-to one relationships, more counselling and personal development*
4.4 *Write down the skills on the model furthest away from the shape of your profile. These are likely to be the skills that you find most difficult:*	*Clarifying roles, monitoring progress and specifying targets and standards*

The 'Change' skills that you have highlighted on the model can also be added. If they are the same ones as you have already written down, underline them as being particularly significant – you may decide that these are the ones you want to concentrate on first. In the example 'monitoring progress' and 'specifying targets and standards' are likely to be priorities.

*4.4 (continued) Add the high-
     lighted 'Change' skills,
     underlining any on page
     38 that are the same:*

                                              Planning action

*How committed are you to
improving these skills?*

                                                      *Very -
                          I __must__ get things better organized - quickly!*

5. Personal development plan

In the examples in Sections 4.4 'clarifying roles' and 'setting targets and standards' are covered by this workbook, and so these two skills can be developed with the help of the skills pages which follow. 'Monitoring progress' is covered in Volume 4, *Managing Resources.*

The person with the profile on page 35 may therefore decide, in addition to the skills in this workbook, to develop the other skills in Volume 4, 'making decisions' and 'persuading' in addition to 'monitoring progress', which has already been highlighted as a 'Change' skill.

The model of the skills in each volume of the Manager's Toolkit series on page 13 is reproduced on page 40 as an ongoing reference at the start of the skills pages.

You will observe, as you move through the skills pages, that at the end of each chapter a model shows the skills in the Manager's Toolkit which most closely relate to the particular skills in this book.

A logical development plan might be to move next to the *Managing People* skills in volume 2 of the series, which, you will see from pages 58, 74 and 94, link to all of the skills in this volume. However, for the person whose Profile appears on page 35, *their natural strengths already lie in that area.*

We have seen that 'monitoring progress' has been identified in Section 4.4 as a 'Change' skill. On page 58 you will see that 'making decisions' and 'persuading' from *Managing Resources* link to 'clarifying roles'. On page 74 'monitoring progress' and 'making decisions link to 'specifying targets and standards'. In view of the shape of the individual's Profile and 'Change' requirements, *Managing Resources* may be a more worthwhile next step.

The 'Operations' skills of clarifying roles, specifying targets and standards and planning action now follow, with explanations on the left and practice activities on the right.

Chapter Two

CLARIFYING ROLES

1. Having a purpose   Page 42

2. Giving it shape   Page 44

3. Writing it down   Page 48

4. Talking it over   Page 52

5. Summary worksheets   Page 54

6. Links to other skills   Page 58

CLARIFYING ROLES

Clarifying roles helps you and your team get your work into perspective so that you can realistically assess the priorities of your operation and work effectively with each other and your customers.

1. Having a purpose

Whenever we have to do something it is helpful if we know *why* we have to do it. Whether at work or at home we operate with more enthusiasm if we know the *purpose* behind what we are supposed to be doing. Why does the organization need this particular job done? Why does the Cricket Club need a chairman? You may even need to consider such fundamentals as what it is that you really want from coming to work or the purpose of your present career.

Individuals and organizations alike can gain great benefit from giving thought to the purpose of each role. Try it for yourself first and then for each of those who report directly to you. Ask them to do the same and then talk through the comparison of what emerges.

With all systematic clarification of work it is important to *write it down*. Try to express in writing the purpose of your job, read what you have written and be willing to amend it freely. You are very unlikely to get it right first time, so be prepared to rewrite it until it represents what your role is really all about. Once you have got it right, the statement you have written will not only give perspective to all you do but will also help you to explain your role to other people.

1. Having a purpose

How clear are you about the purpose of your work, what you are trying to achieve overall?

1.1 Try writing it down:

> *To manage my department effectively*

1.2 Think again – keep altering it until it represents what your role is really all about.

> *To achieve agreed results by providing specialist advice and making most of resources under my control*

2. Giving it shape

Clarifying the purpose of what we do can be beneficially taken further. It is not just a question of *why* we do things, but being clear on *what* we are supposed to be doing. It is remarkable how often people are expected to carry out work without anyone explaining what they are supposed to be doing. It is somehow assumed that they will soon pick it up with a little experience, or those around them will eventually let them into the secret! Meanwhile the person concerned is not working effectively, is confused and is probably in the process of picking up the wrong methods of working.

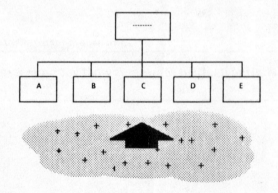

Clarification does not mean that you have to list down *everything* you do – or are supposed to do – that would be bureaucratic and time-consuming. You just need to get all you do into a shape that you and others can visualize. The best approach is to try to structure all you do into about *five headings*, five key areas which together are the significant means by which you achieve the purpose of your job.

2. Giving it shape

Can you visualize a framework for your work to encompass all the things that you do?

2.1 Try developing some headings for the key areas of your role (see pages 54–5):

A ....

PLANNING AND IMPROVING SERVICE AND RESOURCES

B ....

PROVIDING SPECIALIST ADVICE

C ....

CONTROLLING PERFORMANCE

D ....

ORGANIZING

E ....

MOTIVATING STAFF

F ....

2.2 If you find it easier, list all your key activities as shown overleaf, then try to link each with another of a similar type by giving each one an appropriate reference letter. Note that the activities listed are only those that are critical to achieving the main responsibilities of your job. Make a note of the possible headings as they occur to you in Section 2.1 – you can refine them later in Section 2.3 over the page.

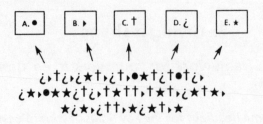

You may be able to create these headings, or most of them, straightaway to provide a meaningful structure. But it is not always that straightforward, and you may find it simpler to list your main activities quickly and roughly, and then try to *sort* them into appropriate headings. Instead of sorting 'top down' by visualizing the headings, you are working 'bottom up', giving shape to what would otherwise appear to be a mass of unrelated day-to-day activities.

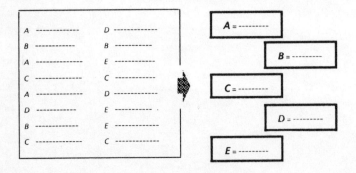

You should now have a purpose for what you do and a shape to the detail of how you achieve that purpose. The next step is to put the headings into priority order, so that you know what are the *most important* areas of activity. This will be very helpful when you have to decide quickly on your priorities, the most important activities that you have to complete.

2.2 (continued) LIST OF KEY ACTIVITIES:

2.3 Write the headings from Section 2.1 (or from your sorting of the activities in Section 2.2) in order of priority. If you are not sure of the relative importance, ask your boss, customer or other appropriate person(s):

1 ....

PLANNING AND IMPROVING SERVICE AND RESOURCES

2 ....

PROVIDING SPECIALIST ADVICE

3 ....

ORGANIZING

4 ....

MOTIVATING STAFF

5 ....

CONTROLLING PERFORMANCE

6 ....

Sometimes it is quite difficult to decide the relative importance of one aspect of your work compared with another. Reference to the purpose may help, ie deciding which group of activities contributes most to the purpose you have defined. If you are still uncertain, try talking to those involved in that particular aspect of your work. Certainly you should consult your boss, and the views of internal and external customers can be very revealing!

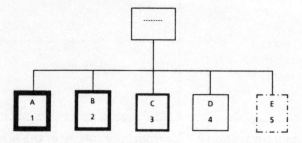

3. Writing it down

You should now have a clear picture of your role, why you do it and the most important aspects of it. The broad framework of purpose and headings in priority order may be sufficient to give you that perspective. But you may find that adding activities and tasks and creating a written format – a *worksheet* – helps to complete the picture. The format can also help to provide a picture of your role to those with whom you come into contact in your work.

In sorting the key headings for your role you probably have already listed your most significant activities. You may now like to add these to the Role Clarification Worksheet on pages 56–7 under the respective headings. You are likely to end up with a structure that has approximately five *activities* under each of approximately five *headings*.

3. Writing it down

Will it help you and other people if you now write it all down on a standard format?

3.1 *Turn to pages 54 and 55 for an example of a completed Role Clarification Worksheet for the role of Specialist Manager. Then turn to pages 56 and 57 where you will find a blank copy for you to build up a worksheet for your own job.*

3.2 *Transfer the purpose of your job from Section 1 and the areas of responsibility from Section 2 to the Role Clarification Worksheet on pages 56–7 in the order of priority that you wrote down in 2.3. above.*

> **PURPOSE:** To achieve the results agreed for my area...
>
> See Section 1.2
>
> | **AREAS OF RESPONSIBILITY:** | A |
> |---|---|
> | PLANNING AND IMPROVING SERVICE AND RESOURCES | |
> | See Section 2.3 for Priority 1 | Priority 2 |

3.3 *Write the day-to-day activities on the worksheet as a result of which you carry out each Area of Responsibility under the appropriate heading. You may have these activities randomly listed in Section 2.2. If they are in the form of nouns, add appropriate verbs:*

> | **AREAS OF RESPONSIBILITY** | A |
> |---|---|
> | **ACTIVITIES** | |
> | - Agree business/customer needs and standards | |
> | - Agree budgets and financial targets. | |

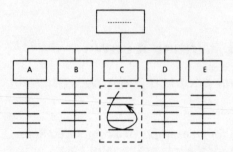

You may start with key nouns, like 'meetings' or 'systems' and then add verbs like 'checking' or 'maintaining'. A combination of specific nouns and verbs will give you the maximum benefit in the shortest time (*MCI Element 1.1*). With the *framework* in place you now have defined the procedure you follow to ensure that each heading is achieved. It is the *maintenance* of this procedure that enables you to satisfy your internal or external customers' specifications on a regular basis.

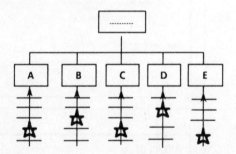

But our work rarely consists of routine activities alone. We also have special things to do which are one-off areas of special attention, special tasks aimed at a particular *improvement*. Once they have been completed they either disappear or become a routine activity that is then added to our role. For example, if we arrange a special meeting to find out what is upsetting a particular customer, we may decide to make it a regular means of customer contact and build it into our normal role.

3.4   List the special improvement tasks or objectives
that you currently have to
achieve, which are
separate from the routine
activities of your role:

....

....

....

....

....

....

....

....

Add these under the
appropriate headings of
the worksheet:

TASK SUMMARIES

Prepare and present report on means
of reducing costs by 7%.

3.5   Do they all fit the structure
of the role that you have
now clarified? If not,
should you be doing that
task?

These special tasks or objectives should fit within the structure of the job that you have now clarified, they should be part of your normal role. If they do not, for example special projects for your own personal development or in response to a particular crisis, there will be no problem for a short period. But if they continue the role may need to be re-defined and developed to take note of them. It is very important that once written down worksheets should be regularly – but *informally* – kept up to date.

4. Talking it over

In all this clarification it is important to note areas of uncertainty and who you need to talk to in order to sort them out. In a team, *gaps or overlaps* in areas of responsibility can easily appear and need to be talked through openly. The completed worksheet can be shown to people with whom you come into regular contact to improve relationships and enhance understanding of your work priorities.

It is a helpful discipline to write at the bottom of each area the internal and external *customers* for whom you are carrying out the activities and tasks listed in that area. You can then develop a dialogue with each of them to agree the standards which will ensure on-going customer satisfaction (see Chapter Three).

Time-consuming though all this clarification may seem, the results of *not* clarifying the work we do are considerably more wasteful in the long run in terms of misdirected effort, critical activities not carried out or long-standing rivalries over 'who does what'. And remember, as managers of others how else are we going to be able to monitor and appraise the on-going work of our staff?

4. Talking it over

Is your role clear to and agreed by the key people with whom you come into contact?

4.1 How clear are you about the identity of your internal or external customers and the standards they require? *Try adding them under the appropriate heading of the worksheet.*	**CUSTOMERS** Accounts Dept
4.2 Are there any possible gaps in your work or overlaps with other people's work?	*Budget guidelines are issued by Accounts*
4.3 Identify the action you need to take to clarify your customers, standards, gaps, overlaps etc	*Check with Accounts*
4.4 Who could benefit from understanding your role better and how could you let them know?	*Copy to each team member and discuss at our next meeting*

ROLE CLARIFICATION WORKSHEET

PURPOSE: *To achieve the results agreed for my area of responsibility by providing specialist advice and making the most of the resources under my control.*

AREAS OF RESPONSIBILITY **A**	**B**	**C**
PLANNING AND IMPROVING SERVICE AND RESOURCES	*PROVIDING SPECIALIST ADVICE*	*ORGANIZING*
ACTIVITIES - *Agree business/'customer' needs and targets.* - *Agree budgets and financial targets.* - *Constantly seek and recommend as appropriate ways of improving service and performance.* - *Be aware of developments in use of facilities, systems, equipment etc and recommend improvements when justified.* - *Prepare written plans and reports as required, keeping contingencies under review.*	- *Maintain dialogue with internal and external 'customers' to ensure relevance of advice/service.* - *Keep up-to-date with specialism through contacts, reading and appropriate training.* - *Assist staff in resolving specialist problems.* - *Contribute to development of appropriate policy, procedures and inter-departmental requirements.*	- *Define organizational needs and clarify roles.* - *Recruit, select and train staff to meet organizational needs.* - *Encourage effective support from other sections/services.* - *Take appropriate decisions to ensure that results are actually achieved.* - *Manage own time effectively seeking opportunities to delegate as appropriate.*
TASK SUMMARIES *Prepare and present report on means of reducing costs by 7%.*	*Respond more quickly to customers' requirements.*	*Recruit replacement for Jane Rogers by 30 June.*
CUSTOMERS *A-Z Cos/customers, middle managers, Accounts Dept, boss*	*A-Z Cos/customers, middle managers, staff, boss*	*Staff and boss*

TITLE: *SPECIALIST MANAGER*

	D	E	F
	MOTIVATING STAFF	*CONTROLLING PERFORMANCE*	

D	E	F
- *Keep staff informed of business/customer needs, and agree tasks, priorities and standards.* - *Encourage contribution of ideas for improvement individually or in groups.* - *Coach, train and develop as appropriate to individual and business needs.* - *Within budget and policy constraints ensure staff are and believe themselves to be fairly remunerated.* - *Resolve issues promptly, minimizing effects of adverse personal problems.*	- *Establish and maintain effective means of monitoring performance.* - *Make most of available systems support.* - *Personally review individual performance on regular basis.* - *Ensure policies and procedures (incl. Health and Safety) are adhered to.* - *Take appropriate action to put things right.*	Use only if a role has six Areas of Responsibility
Produce departmental training and development plan by year end.	*Simplify method of monthly reporting.*	
Staff	*Staff, boss and appropriate customers*	

© *PETER GRAINGER 1994*

ROLE CLARIFICATION WORKSHEET

PURPOSE:

AREAS OF RESPONSIBILITY A	B	C
ACTIVITIES		
TASK SUMMARIES		
CUSTOMERS		

TITLE:

	D	E	F

Clarifying Roles
links to other skills in
the Manager's Toolkit series

Each skill in this book not only links directly with the other 'operations' skills in the book (3 and 6), but also with other skills from the toolkit on page 13 (8, 9, 11 and 12).

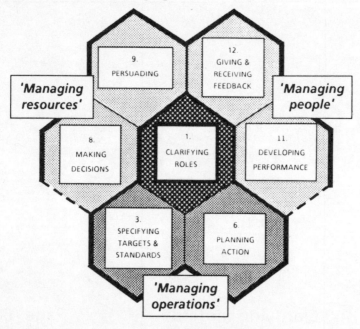

Decision-making (8) frequently accompanies the process of role clarification in the systematic selection of personnel, and persuasion (9) may be required before a person accepts a particular position or part of a role.

Giving and receiving feedback (12) should be carried out in the context of the person's whole job, while the development of performance depends on an appreciation of the person's total role and consideration of possible future positions.

Chapter Three

SPECIFYING TARGETS AND STANDARDS

1. Clarifying targets   Page 60

2. Defining standards   Page 64

3. Involving others   Page 66

4. Summary worksheets   Page 70

5. Links to other skills   Page 74

SPECIFYING TARGETS AND STANDARDS

Specifying targets and standards ensures that you know precisely what you and others are supposed to be doing and can then effectively monitor your progress.

1. Clarifying targets

Whether clarifying roles or agreeing operational specifications, we end up sooner or later with the need for *clearly defined* action. Whether this action emerges from an organizational structure or is a task placed on us by someone else, it needs to be clearly defined to ensure that we know precisely what we have to achieve.

The critical step is to be able to define the activity or task as an 'end result' target, a situation that we can actually envisage, something almost tangible. A particularly helpful way to acquire this skill is to compare it with making a journey. When we set out on a journey we envisage arriving at a particular *destination* – the journey is not complete until we actually arrive at that destination. It is the same with a target or objective, for example if we decide

> *to drive to the Skyline Hotel at Heathrow to meet John Drew at reception by 11.00 am on 25 April,*

we shall clearly know whether or not we have met our target.

1. Clarifying targets

Do you know precisely what you are trying to achieve with each activity or task you currently have underway?

1.1 Identify a significant activity from your normal work (consider your Role Clarification Worksheet on pages 56–7) or an important special task you have to carry out in the next few months (see page 51, Section 3.4):

> *To move office next month*

1.2 In comparison, think of the last journey of any length that you went on. Write down the precise destination and purpose of that journey.

> *To drive to my parents home in time for lunch at 1.00 pm. on Sunday*

Would you have known, from what you have written, the precise point of arrival?

1.3 Try to rewrite the activity or task in 1.1 in a way that describes the situation when it has actually been achieved, ie the precise destination you are trying to reach (the end result).

> *To arrange for the removal of my office equipment to the new block by end of May*

The words you use should describe the result you are trying to achieve, the destination you are aiming to arrive at. The target will not have been achieved until you cross the boundary and shake the hand of the person you travelled to meet. The test is, how will you know when you have arrived, when you have actually reached the destination?

Defining the destination clarifies the 'what', but the target is not adequately specified until the 'who', 'when', 'where', 'how much' etc are added. If *you* are taking the action, who are you doing it *to*, and *when* is it to be done by? Who are you meeting and at what time? Where are you going to meet and what facilities or equipment are going to be needed? *Why* should be clear as a result of clarifying the purpose of your role (see page 43).

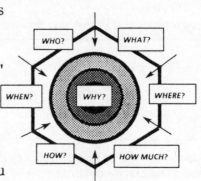

'Who' leads you to clarifying the relationship between the 'supplier' – the person who completes the action or output – and the 'customer' who receives the completed action. It's rather like a three-quarter line in rugby football with each internal customer passing something tangible on to the next until it reaches the external customer – the winger who scores the try!

Sometimes internal customers add something to what we pass to them, and then pass it back to us. We then become *their* customer.

1.4 Now consider who are you going to 'supply' the task to (ie your customer). When is it to be done by, and where or with what resources? Is there a limit to the resources you have available?

WHO TO?		

WHEN BY?	WHERE AND WITH WHAT?	HOW MUCH?
		3 quotes from external removers if can't be handled internally
Removal to be completed by 24 May	To 2nd floor front office Packing cases	

1.5 Now rewrite the task or activity in Section 1.3 as a target statement which incorporates all the aspects you have noted above. Are you clearer now on what you are trying to achieve?

I'll arrange with Facilities Dept for the removal of all my current office equipment to the second floor front office in the new block. The move is to be completed by 24 May so that I can be fully operational by the end of the month. I will need packing cases in advance from Facilities Dept, and quotations from external removal firms if Facilities cannot meet deadline.

'Where' is not always significant, but the checklist ensures you don't miss anything important. As soon as you think about a location, what is actually in that location comes to mind: equipment, materials, systems, etc which will help you to meet the target. We are talking of *resources* ('with what?'), and with this of course comes consideration of the *cost and quantity* of those resources ('how much').

When all this information has been considered, you are in a position to define the target or objective in full. The more precise the definition of the target the easier it is to be sure you or members of your team have actually achieved it. Shooting at a target that keeps moving or is shrouded in uncertainty has no guarantee of accuracy – or satisfaction!

2. Defining standards

However, real accuracy and satisfaction only come with the addition of standards or measures of performance. Standards and measurement are often seen as negative and restrictive, but are in reality great motivators. Just as we like to know how our journey is progressing – 'how much further?' – so we like to know how we are doing in achieving our targets. If we can agree the standards required with a customer to whom we are giving, as it were, a *personal service*, our motivation will be even stronger.

Most targets have a *time* standard, the date the task has to be completed by. But is it *precise*? Is completion due at the beginning or end of the day, month or year? Is there an assumption that you know when, or is it simply required 'as soon as possible'? The great advantage of time standards is that they are generally measurable – calendars, clocks and even stop-watches are readily available!

2. Defining standards

Do you find it easy to know how well you are doing?

2.1 *Look back to the task or activity that you have just clarified and check how many standards you have included as measures of your performance.*

2.2 Have you included a time standard, ie the date by which the task should have been completed? If not, write a time standard here:	*I will notify them by 30 April*
2.3 Identify any of the standards that are essential, ie minimum standards below which you cannot afford to drop? *Are they actually measurable?* *If not, are they really essential or could you make them measurable?* *Rewrite any standards that really are essential to make sure that they are measurable:*	*Must try Facilities dept first; must give four weeks' notice; select cheapest of 3 quotes.*

Some standards, of course, are not actually measurable and therefore lose their benefit as methods of motivation or control. The priority is to make sure that the *essential* standards are measurable, the minimum level below which you simply cannot afford to drop. Relevant Health and Safety regulations, for example, should be included among your essential standards (*MCI Element 1.2*).

Because essential standards really do represent the minimum acceptable level, you are unlikely to have more than three or four for any one target. It is worth checking through each of your current targets to determine whether any of your current standards really are *essential*.

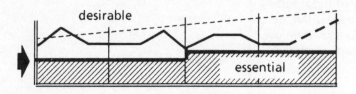

If we accept that standards, particularly if agreed with a customer, can be motivational, setting additional or more challenging standards can actually stimulate results by giving ourselves, and others, something additional to aim at – provided of course that they are seen to be reasonable and achievable.

3. Involving others

Consideration of tasks and standards leads inevitably to delegation and the key question, *is it really essential that you do it?* Another person may not do it as well as you – initially – but it could be an important development opportunity for them, as well as giving you more time for other things.

2.4 Look again at the who?, where?, when?, how much? in 1.4. Try adding new standards so that you have something more challenging to aim at.	*I could notify them three days earlier*
2.5 Have you as the 'supplier' talked over the standards required with your 'customer'? If not, how could you make sure it happens ?	*Talk to Facilities about feasibility if giving short notice*

3. Involving others

How good are you at getting things done through the work of other people?

3.1 Look again at the task you clarified in 1.5. Is it essential for you to do it, or every part of it? If not who could you delegate it to?	*Dept Secretary could make the arrangements*

When you are specifying targets and standards for someone else as part of your management role, you will need to give careful thought to how you are going to ensure their commitment to the work you want done. You may appreciate the importance of the task, but will they?

A sure way to encourage commitment to what you want done is to consult the other person on the standards and methods that will be required. How far are you able or prepared to *consult*?

When you involve others in agreeing targets and standards they are likely to have their own views on how the task is to be achieved and the standards that they consider achievable – often suggesting more challenging standards or better methods than you have in mind.

And remember that specific end result targets and standards are critical to *monitoring* progress and keeping control of the delegated task. You can delegate with confidence if *both* of you have agreed the precise result to be achieved. It takes longer but you can be much more assured of the result.

As you get other people working on a range of tasks you are in danger of losing control of the *progress* of each of them. The Team Worksheet on 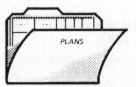 pages 72–3 enables you to keep a note of the complexity of the tasks under your control, the key action steps for each, who is responsible as supplier, who is the customer, the date for completion and how each end result is going to be measured. It can also be used to enable individuals to keep a note of their own separate tasks for which planning worksheets have not yet been completed (see pages 92–3).

3.2 How are you going to get their commitment to do it to the standards the customer requires, eg how far are you prepared to consult them about what is required, and how it is to be achieved?	*Ask for help and explain pressure of other deadlines*
3.3 Identify a task that you require someone else to carry out: Proceed through steps 1.3 to 2.5, specifying the target and standards for that 'supplier':	*Discuss target, standards and methods of meeting them tomorrow*
3.4 Consider how you are going to communicate, monitor and control the progress made against the agreed target and standards:	*Agree individually and review at monthly meeting*

3.5 Transfer that and other delegated tasks onto the Team Review Work-sheet which follows on pages 72–3 adding how you plan to monitor their performance.

You can also note down all your own unrelated tasks on this work-sheet so that you can monitor your own performance.

NAME/SECTION/DEPARTMENT: *Specialist Manager* (See Role Clarification)		**TEAM REVIEW WORKSHEET**
ROLE REF. No.	TASK	KEY ACTION STEPS
A	*Prepare and present 7% cost reduction report*	
		1. Review current spend with section leaders
		2. Generate ideas on cost reduction
		3. Develop ideas with section leaders
B	*Respond more quickly to customers' requirements*	
		1. Make staff aware of need to improve 'customer care'
		2. Check current methods of dealing with customers and agree guidelines
		3. Improve clarity of customers' requirements
		4. Develop others' ability to help
C	*Recruit Jane's replacement*	
		1. Submit requisition and specification
		2. Supply candidates from advert
		3. Select and appoint

DATE: *30 April 1994*

SUPPLIER	(INTERNAL) CUSTOMER	COMPLETION DATE	METHOD OF MONITORING
Me	*Boss*	*15 Sept*	*Presentation of written plan*
Section leaders	*Me*	*31 May*	*Figures of sect spend for last 3 yrs and plans*
All staff	*Me via section leaders*	*30 June*	*Check developing list – all to be involved*
etc...			
Me and staff	*All customers*	*31 Dec*	*Weekly schedule of nos and time taken*
Me	*Staff*	*30 Nov*	*Positive response to feedback at team mtgs*
Liz	*Me*	*15 June*	*Consolidated report and guidelines meeting*
Me/staff	*All customers*	*16 Sept*	*Written requirements from 75% of customers*
etc...			
Me and Personnel Officer		*30 June*	*Confirm applicant's starting date*
Me with Jane	*Personnel Officer*	*15 May*	*Jane to check progress*
Personnel Officer	*Me*	*15 June*	*Shortlist of three if possible*
etc...			© *PETER GRAINGER 1994*

NAME/SECTION/DEPARTMENT:

TEAM REVIEW WORKSHEET

ROLE REF. No.	TASK	KEY ACTION STEPS

DATE: SHEET NUMBER:

SUPPLIER	(INTERNAL) CUSTOMER	COMPLETION DATE	METHOD OF MONITORING

Specifying Targets and Standards
links to other skills in the Manager's Toolkit series

Each skill in this book not only links directly with the other 'operations' skills in the book (1 and 6), but also with other skills from the toolkit on page 13 (2, 4, 8 and 10).

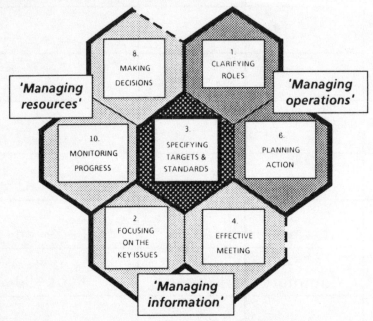

Performance can only be effectively monitored (10) if end result targets and standards have been defined and agreed, while essential and desirable standards are the basis of the criteria for systematic decision-making (8).

An appreciation of the relevant targets and standards helps to focus on an issue (2), as well as adding precision to the solution. Meetings are frequently not effective (4) because targets and standards have not been set, while meetings themselves are means of sharing team targets and standards.

Chapter Four

PLANNING ACTION

1. Identifying options   Page 76

2. Making it visible   Page 80

3. Setting priorities   Page 82

4. Making it happen   Page 86

5. Summary worksheets   Page 90

6. Links to other skills   Page 94

PLANNING ACTION

Planning action converts a range of initial unformed options into a written plan for appropriate action by an individual or team.

1. Identifying options

Creating a plan of action so that you and others involved know how you are going to reach your target is only necessary if the action consists of *a number* of steps. A single step to reach your goal scarcely requires 'planning'. You need a number of action steps and therefore a number of options. Without a range of options your plan will be limited and so less likely to succeed.

By consulting other people you are likely to receive additional ideas on *how* the task should be achieved, and these may be sufficient. But if the task is something that has needed improvement over many years new ideas may not emerge quite so readily. You may therefore need techniques to stimulate those thoughts.

The easiest to use, individually or with a group, is based on identifying as many factors as possible that could *help or hinder* the achievement of the task. Not only is this a very visual technique – ideal for use with a flipchart – but it enables you to identify a surprising range of potential resources and potential risks to your plan at a very early stage. If you use the 'who, what, where, when' checklist from page 62 further ideas will emerge.

1. Identifying options

Do you need to have additional ideas on how to achieve a task?

1.1 Write down the target for which you want additional options:

To get need for customer care across to my staff

1.2 List all the factors which could possibly help or hinder the achievement of that target.	POTENTIAL HELPS	POTENTIAL HINDERS
	Boss very keen, recent conference...	*Low morale, Jane's leaving...*

It is important to let the factors occur to you randomly and not to limit yourself in any way at this stage; the method of prioritizing later in this chapter (pages 82–5) will help you to identify the most important.   They are likely to be nouns or adjectives – leave out verbs for the moment.

To help you or your team extend your ideas you could try freeing up your thinking by not letting anyone criticize or disagree with any suggestions. As with 'brainstorming' (see Making More of Others' Ideas' in Volume 2, *Managing People*), write down any factor that helps on the left or hinders on the right as they arise. Try not to let the process get bogged down with too much clarifying of the meaning of each factor.

If you have more than six or so factors on each side of the page group them together by similar type, just as you did in clarifying the activities of your role (see pages 44–7), by adding an appropriate letter to each until a reasonable structure has emerged.

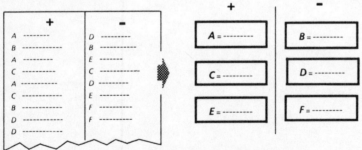

You should now have some positive headings, such as 'Help from boss', for the factors on the left, and negative headings on the right, for example 'System inadequate'. They should still be nouns at this stage, because the next step is to think of ways of *maximizing* the helps on the left and *minimizing* the hinders on the right. Words like 'develop' or 'overcome' will spring to mind as the basis of a draft action plan.

1.3   Try to link each factor on the left in Section 1.2 with another of a similar
      type by giving each an appropriate letter, until you have three or four
      headings on each side. Write down the headings, still keeping the
      positive and negative factors separate:

A. *Others are doing it*	E. *Clash of other priorities*
B. *Senior management committed*	F. *Little personal contact*
C. *Essential to our business now*	G. *Seen as 'flavour of the month'*
D. 	H.

1.4   Write down ways of maximizing the key potential help factors and of
      minimizing the key potential hinder factors in 1.3.

....

A. Find out what other companies are doing.

....

B. Maximize senior management's commitment.

....

C. Explain the business need.

....

E. Make sure it is given priority.

....

F. Provide opportunities for more personal customer contact.

....

G. Overcome staff's cynicism to 'just another programme'.

2. Making it visible

Your plan at this stage probably has steps but no shape or time sequence. A plan should at least determine 'who' is to do 'what' by 'when', and the 'when' cannot be defined until the main steps are placed in a sequence. Have a look at the steps or options in whatever form they are available to you, and see if you can see a natural sequence which will lead from where you are now to where you want to be when your overall target is achieved.

$$\boxed{1} \rightarrow \boxed{2} \rightarrow \boxed{3} \rightarrow \boxed{4} \rightarrow \boxed{5} \rightarrow \boxed{6}$$

It is now time to construct your plan so that you and others involved have something visible to work with. Write down the sequence of steps as target statements within the framework of your original main target. Transfer these on to the 'Planning Worksheet' (see example on pages 90–1) and add who is to do what to whom, by when, where and with the aid of what equipment etc (see 'Specifying targets and standards', page 62).

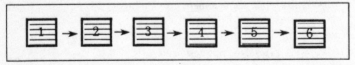

Complete each section, if appropriate, as a reminder of what resources you are going to need. Are you likely to be short of any of these resources? If so, be creative about *potential resources*, just as you were in Section 1 about potential help factors. Are you making the best use of all the factors you listed then? (*MCI Elements 6.1– 6.3.*)

2. Making it visible

Do you need to assemble your proposed actions into a visible plan for you and/or others to follow?

2.1   What is your plan setting out to achieve? Write down the overall target from Section 1.1:

> *To make sure that all my staff are fully aware of the need for improved customer care by end Nov*

2.2   Write down the four most important action steps in an appropriate sequence as target statements (see 1.4 on page 79):

1.

> *Agree draft plan with boss to ensure his commitment to customer care priorities, more personal contacts with customers and other companies and attending my staff meeting*

2.

> *Include customer care item on agenda of team meetings, incorporating explanation of business need, information on other companies, and proposals for visiting key customers*

3.

> *Arrange customer contact programme*

4.

> *Make sure that customer care really is given appropriate priority by me and my boss*

3. Setting priorities

To make sure our plans succeed we have to make sure that their priority elements are safeguarded, not only against other less important aspects of the plan itself but also against all the other activities and tasks that form part of our on-going job. But how do we determine which are the *priority* steps, activities or tasks? Which ones, if we run out of time, must we complete at all costs?

First you need to be very clear precisely what you mean by each of the options you are comparing – particularly important when a *group* is determining its priorities. It is helpful to have each agreed definition written down so that you can refer back to it during the comparisons.

To judge the relative *importance* of each action systematically you will probably need to consider each option against some basic criteria. There are four criteria which are particularly helpful in determining priorities:

- The first, **'Accountability'**, checks how far *you* are specifically responsible for each action. It may be entirely up to you to take the action, you may need help from others, you may need to persuade someone else of the need for action, or you may not be sure how much freedom to act you actually have (see 'Clarifying roles').

- The second criterion is **'Commitment'**, which recognizes the fact that we are more ready to get on with things that we *want* to do, and to see through to the end things that we

2.3   Are you clear who is going to do what to whom, when, where and
       with what equipment for each of the steps? Complete the Plan-
       ning Worksheet on pages 92–3 by adding all your action steps
       in sequence to create a visible plan of action to be followed.

2.4   Are you likely to be short of resources? Note them here and list possible
       alternatives you can think of. Are any of the factors in Section 1.2
       capable of development? Add key ones to the plan.

RESOURCES AT RISK	POSSIBLE ALTERNATIVES
Jane's leaving	*Ensure successor's* *immediate commitment by early involvement*

3.   Setting priorities

*Is there a chance you will not be able to carry out all the steps of
your plan together with all the other tasks and activities you have
to do?*

3.1   Consider the most important parts of your plan, your current tasks and
       the key activities of your job. Write down the actions which are most
       likely to be competing for your time:

A	C	E
Move office	*Recruitment*	*Awareness of customer care*

B	D	F
Integrate staff	*Review current spend*	*Customer contact programme*

enjoy doing. 'Heart' can subtly influence our consider-
ations of both options and factors.

- Next we come to **'Risk'**. This criterion is more difficult
because it contains two opposite elements. The first is the
risk of *not* doing something – what could go wrong as a
result of our *in*action. Where there is a high risk in *not*
doing something, you have a high priority option.

  The second dimension to 'Risk' is the risk of *taking* the
  action, eg the cost, the uncertainty, the likely opposition
  from some people, resource standards that could be
  threatened by *taking* the action. This dimension may
  require you to modify your initial scores, balancing the
  risk of *doing* with that of *not doing* each.

- Last comes **'Opportunity'** or the opposite of 'Risk'. This is
the consideration of the short and long-term *benefits* to be
gained from taking one option rather than another. The
benefits could include the impact of an option on the task
as a whole, the knock-on effect of one option on another or
the impact of one option on your job as a whole.

The four initial letters form a useful mnemonic – **'ACRO'**,
from the Greek for the highest or top.

It can be very helpful to score the options against each of
these criteria by drawing up a lined
matrix. Use a scale of 1 to 5, scoring
each option criterion by criterion.
The quickest approach is to score the
highest option first as a benchmark
and then compare the other options
with it. The scores are then added
up and a priority rating given to each option.

	A	B	C	D	E	F
A						
C						
R						
O						
Tot.						

3.2   Are you quite certain what you mean by each of these actions? If not,
      rewrite the wording of each option so that you will be able to compare
      them precisely:

A	C	E
Move my office by 24 June	Recruit Jane's replacement	Make staff aware of need for improved customer care

B	D	F
Integrate Bill's staff into my section	Identify recent spend and validate resource plans	Arrange customer contact programme

3.3 Score each option on a five-point scale (5 = 'High'; 1 = 'Low') against each
     of the following criteria in turn:

OPTIONS:	A	B	C	D	E	F
ACCOUNTABILITY How far is it your responsibility to see each option through?	4	5	4	4	5	3
COMMITMENT How much do you personally want to take each action ?	4	4	4	3	5	3
RISK What are the risks in _not_ doing each? Should you adjust the scores because there are risks involved in doing each?	4	4	5	4	4	3
OPPORTUNITY What are the immediate and long-term benefits to be gained from each option?	4	5	4	4	5	5
3.4 Add up the total score for each option and identify the resulting priority rating: **TOTAL:**	16	18	17	15	19	14
Add priorities to worksheets. **PRIORITY RATING:**	4	2	3	5	1	6

4. Making it happen

Now that you have a visible plan and you know your priorities, how much does your plan depend on other people? Do you need to make it visible to anyone who is involved in the action steps you have identified? You may need to consult them on the content before you finalize it – they are much more likely to be committed to their part in it if you do!

Remember that having a plan that is structured, defined and visible not only enables you to monitor your own and others' performance, but, given their commitment to it, enables others to take responsibility for monitoring *their own performance*.

Many plans for improvement stop at this point, prepared, written down, communicated and then assigned to a file or desk. Operational planning is about making things happen – consistently. Often so much effort goes into planning that we have nothing left to make it actually happen.

Personal style plays an important part in how good we are at seeing our plans through. Look back at your own Style Profile (see page 37), and remind yourself of the shape of your triangle.

'Command' people are particularly good at getting things done, seeing what needs doing and getting on with it. However they don't always manage to take other people with them. 'Bond' people are very good at working with others and keeping the team together, but are not so good at actually getting results on time.

4. Making it happen

Are you good at making plans actually happen?

4.1 Do you need to let other people know of all or part of your plan or be consulted on any part of it?	*Meetings with boss, customers and staff - colleagues may be interested*
Who needs to be consulted and how will you tell them about it?	*Meetings with boss, customers*
4.2 What does your personal Style Profile tell you about your ability to get others to work enthusiastically with you? Look particularly at the 'Bond' dimension:	*I'm better working with individuals than with groups at meetings*
4.3 If you need to get others' commitment to your plan, how are you going to do it?	*Prepare ground carefully before seeing my boss and show more enthusiasm to boss and staff*
4.4 What does your personal Style Profile tell you about your ability to make things happen? Look particularly at the 'Command' dimension:	*I'm better at thinking about what has to be done than in making sure that it actually gets done*

If we are to make our plan an *action* plan, we have to breathe life into it – we have to 'manage' it. Managing requires enthusiasm and energy, attributes which require individual effort and a *positive attitude* of mind – 'positive Pygmalion' – turned into action (see page 26).

If you look again at the section on personal style (page 30), you will see the definition of **'Drive'** style. Consider yourself in relation to the description. Do you have a clear vision of what needs to be done and are you positive about what is possible? Are you capable of generating enthusiasm in others? How flexible are you about the means of achieving your plans? Can you react positively to circumstances and to new ideas?

Most plans require the involvement of other people and people are motivated not only by enthusiasm and vision, but by sensitivity towards themselves as human beings, their feelings and their needs. Motivation is achieved as much by 'Heart' as by 'Head' and 'Feet'. Teamwork involves caring for each team member as a person, being open and responsive to each member as a valued *individual*. Respond positively to them and they will respond with positive results to you.

Having taken stock of your own personal style you are now in a position to stand back and review the reliability of your plans. If in reviewing those plans you identify risks to any part, think about overcoming them and add those actions to the plan. You are in effect minimizing potential 'hinder' factors. It is sensible to consider 'contingency plans' for all your tasks as the steps for completing each of them emerge.

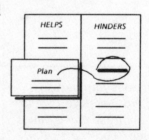

4.5 The 'DRIVE' dimension is a combination of the other three styles. Try scoring yourself against the 'Drive' criteria:

	Always	Usually	Some-times	Rarely
Clear and positive in thinking towards future possibilities.		✓		
Capable of generating enthusiasm in others.			✓	
Capable of a flexible approach to achieving results.		✓		
Sensitive to others' feelings and expectations.		✓		
Inspire teamwork.				✓

4.6 In view of the priorities you identified in 3.3 and your ability to ensure commit-ment in 4.4, consider the risks associated with each step of your plan on pages 92–3):

Availability of Jane, Jim and boss, pressure of time

Look back at the potential hinder factors in 1.2 to make sure you haven't missed anything.

I may get an adverse reaction

Identify additional steps to try to overcome the risks and add them to your plans.

Involve Jane's replacement quickly, get boss's commitment early

PLANNING WORKSHEET

PURPOSE or OVERALL TARGET:

SEQUENCE AND PRIORITY		TARGETS (specific end result of each step)	SUPPLIER
2	2	Prepare draft plan to include prioritizing, client and company contacts and staff meetings, and then...	Me with Jim
3	2	discuss and agree final plan with boss, including info on business need.	Me
1	5	Jane and Jim to assemble info on examples of poor 'customer care', good Co examples and key clients.	Jane and Jim
4	1	Include customer care item on agenda of our Team Meetings (plan intro and then regular discussion).	Me
5	4	Ensure customer care given appropriate priority.	Me and boss
6	3	Arrange visits of key staff to clients and examples of good company practice and...	Me
7	3	implement client and company visits for key staff.	Jim and Jane's
8	6	Review progress and development of staff's attitude.	Me

*To make sure that my staff are fully aware of the need for
improved 'customer care' by 30 November (Task 'B1', Page 70)*   SHEET NUMBER: *1*

(INTERNAL) CUSTOMER	COMPLETION DATE	RESOURCES REQUIRED	POSSIBLE RISKS
Jane will type key elements	30 June	Planning worksheet Co and client info	Close to Jane's leaving date
Boss (+ some colleagues?)	14 July	Typed draft plan and back-up info	Availability of boss?
Me	15 June	Information from all	Their availability?
All direct reports	20 July	Summary of plan and back-up info	
All direct reports and customers	from 20 July	Guidelines to be agreed with boss	Will mean a change of style!
Key clients and Co contacts	15 September	Phone and written confirmation	Time – they'll be too busy!
Staff agreed by me	On-going from July	Agreed schedule and reports back to me	Staff out of action too long
All direct reports	15 November	Review of reports, special meeting	Have no method of measuring results

PLANNING WORKSHEET

PURPOSE or OVERALL TARGET:

SEQUENCE AND PRIORITY	TARGETS (specific end result of each step)	SUPPLIER

SHEET NUMBER:

(INTERNAL) CUSTOMER	COMPLETION DATE	RESOURCES REQUIRED	POSSIBLE RISKS
			© *PETER GRAINGER 1994*

Planning Action
links to other skills in
the Manager's Toolkit series

Each skill in this book not only links directly with the other 'operations' skills in the book (1 and 3), but also with other skills from the toolkit on page 13 (4, 5, 7 and 11).

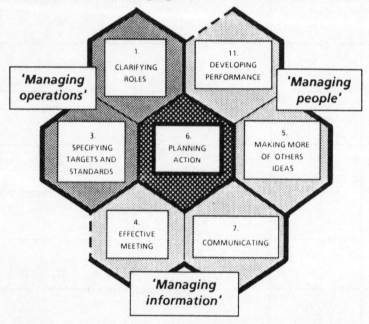

When planning action, the knowledge of the capabilities and potential of your team, which comes from regularly developing performance (11), is critical, and the options available to you will be significantly enhanced by making more of others' ideas (5).

Your plan will need to be communicated to others (7) and discussed (4) to develop the action and ensure commitment.

Index

bold type denotes main references

accountability/responsibility 8, 16, 19
    45, 49, 52, 54-7, 82, 85
Acland, Roger 6
'ACRO' 82-85
activities/routines 12, 16, 45-51, 78,
    82-3
'Analyse' 28-31, 33-35, 37
attitude/expectations, positive 6, 9,
    24-7, 30, 88-9, 90 *see also*
    Pygmalion Effect
'Bond' 28-31, 33-35, 37
client use of approach 5, 6
'Command' 28-31, 33-5, 37, 86, 87
commitment 14, 39, 68-69, 79, 82, 83,
    85, 86, 87, 89, 94
communicating 18, 30, 34, 69, 86, 94
confidence 24, 26, 34, 68
contingency planning 14, 18, 54, 88
control 14, 66, 68-9
cost 22, 54, 64, 70
criteria 74, 82, 84-5
customer **52-7**
    care 70, 77, 81, 83, 85, 90-1
    contact 18, 25, 50, 62-3, 69, 79, 87
    identification 52-7, 65-7, 63, 68,
    71, 73, 91, 93
    requirements 22, 23, 47, 48, 54,
    55, 64, 67, 70-1
decision 16, 39, 40, 54, 58, 74
delegating 54, 66-9
development, personal **Ch 1, 21-40**,
    aids 10, 19, 21, 24, 28, 30-1, 58
    MCI and management 14, 15, 16
    opportunities 23, 38, 52, 55, 66
    plan 9, 28-9, 34, 36, 38-40, 55, 93

'Drive' 30, 34, 88-9
enthusiasm 22, 26, 30, 42, 88-9
factors, help and hinder 26, 76-9, 80,
    83, 84, 88, 89
feedback 16, 30, 34, 38, 58
groups 22, 24, 32-3, 55, 76, 82, 87
    see also teams
Health and Safety Regulations 55, 66
Huthwaite Research Group 5
ideas 22, 30, 32-3, 34, 38, 55, 70, 76-7,
    78, 88, 94 *see also* options
improvement 14, 16, 17, 50, 51, 54-5,
    76
'Interactive Skills' 5
involvement/consultation 18, 23, 66-9
    76, 80, 83, 86-8
Japan 22
job 22, 27, 29, 42, 44-5, 56, 82, 83, 84
    see also role
Kepner and Tregoe 5
leadership 9, 28, 30
learning, open 6, 10, 12, 18-19, 23
MCI, Management Charter Initiative
    12, **14-17**, 21, 50, 66, 80
methods 15, 16, 44, 55, 66, 68, 78, 91
    see also procedures
monitoring/measurable **64-73**
    as part of plan 71, 73, 86, 91
    profile skill 30, 34, 36, 38
    self monitoring 23, 60, 64, 68-9
    series links 13, 39, 40, 74
    with standards for control 14, 18,
    52, 55, 64-6, 68, 69
motivation 22, 28, 55, 64, 66, 88
objectives 14, 15, 16, 51, 60
    see also tasks and targets

options 16, 76-9, 80, 82-5, 94,
  see also ideas

organization 12, 14, 29, 32-3, 42, 60

persuading 39, 40, 58, 82

plan/planning **Ch 4, 82-100**
  'Toolkit' skill 11, 30-1, 35-7, 39
  'Operations' skill 12, 13-14, 15-17
  40, 74, 84, 94
  safeguarding 71, 82, 88-9
  strengthening 54, 78, 80-1, 86-8
  worksheet 68, 80, 83, 90-3

practice 9, 12, 18, 19

priorities 34, 46, 47, 48, 49, 52, 78-9,
  81, **82-4,** 85, 86, 89, 90, 92

problems/issues 5, 21, 22, 54, 55

procedures 16, 21, 28, 50, 54, 55
  see also methods

process 8, 10-11, 16, 58
  see also techniques

profile 6, 29, 34-6, 37, 38, 40, 86, 87

purpose **42-3,** 44, 46, 48, 49, 54, 56,
  62, 90, 92

'Pygmalion Effect' **24-7,** 88
  see also attitude/expectations

quality 14, 22

questionnaire 30, 32, 33

resources 8, 13, 15, 16, 23, 40, 43, 54,
  63, 64, 76, 80, 91, 93

result 6, 11, 12, 24, 26, 28, 29, 30, 43,
  52, 54, 60-2, 68, 74, 86, 88, 89, 90

review 12, 55, 69-73, 83, 88, 90, 91

risk 21, 76, 83, 84, 88-9, 91, 93

role **Ch 2, 42-58,** 11, 12, 13, 16, 17,
  22-3, 31, 34- 5, 37, 38-9, 40, 45, 62,
  68, 74, 78, 82 *see also* jobs

Shaw, George Bernard 24

standards, management 5, 14-15

standards, performance **Ch 3, 66-80**
  agreeing 23, 52, 53, 67, 69
  for control 18, 64-6, 68-9, 84
  as motivator 23, 64, 66-7 68, 69
  'Operations' skill 12, 13-14, 15,
  39-40
  series links 40, 58, 74, 94
  'Toolkit' skill 9, 11, 30-1, 34-7, 38-9

structure 44, 45, 48, 52, 80

style 5, 6, 9, **28-37,** 86, 88, 89, 91
  see also profile

supplier 62-3, 67, 68, 71, 90, 92

targets **Ch 3, 66-80** *see also* tasks
  consulting 54, 68, 74, 77
  defined 60-4, 66, 68-9, 74
  'Operations' skill 12, 13-14, 16, 58,
  94
  'Toolkit' skill 9, 11, 30-1, 34-7, 38-
  40
  as plan 76, 80-1, 90-3

tasks 16, 22, 51, 52, 54-56, 61, 63, 65,
  66-73, 76-7, 82, 83, 84, 91
  see also targets

team/team work 5 *see also* groups
  action to help 23, 88, 94
  meeting 74, 78, 81, 90
  performance 42, 52, 64, 69-73, 76
  skills of management 11-12, 15, 17
  styles 29, 30, 86, 89

techniques 5, 6, 9, 76

Toolkit, The
  Manager's 5, 6, 10-11, 14-15, 29,
  39, 58
  Personal Development 6, 29-31
  series 5, 8, 10, 13, 14-15, 36

worksheet 18, 19, 48, 49, 51, 52, 53,
  54-7, 61, 68-73, 80, 83, 90-3